GODSEX POETRY
Finding Divine Love in Sex
IANA LAHI

GODSEX POETRY

Published through Spirit Gateways® Publishing
All Rights Reserved
Copyright © 2020 by IANA LAHI

Cover Art Copyright © 2020 by Autumn Skye Morrison

Interior Book Design and Layout by:
www.integrativeink.com

ISBN: 978-1-7326474-9-7 (Paperback Edition)

Library of Congress Control Number: 2020916653

No part of this publication may be reproduced, stored in a retrieval system, or transmitted in any form or by any means electronic, mechanical, photocopying, recording or otherwise, without the written permission of the author or publisher.

ianalahi.com

Dedicated to Lovers
Who Treasure
Exploring the Realms
Of Love
Through Devotion
and
Surrender.

May the Pain of Separation and the Joy of Union
Catapult Your Life
Into Oneness.

You put your lips on my forehead
And lit a Holy lamp
Inside my heart.
— Hafiz

Stay For Good

Meet your heart
So you can meet mine
Anything else is not my design
Find the gateway
Of desire
Let it set your soul
On fire
Become One
With you
Open to allow
Your Self
To see
I have always been standing
Next to you
Waiting for you to see
The love inside of you
You come and go from
As you quickly run away
Stay for good
Become One
In our fire
My love.

Yearn

Take off your protective armor
Come into my bed
Of wild rose petals
And roll into the meadows
Where shadows consumed
By love
Yearn to BE free.

You Are Always There

You are always there
The love you tender
The love you hold
Releases me from self doubt
BEing One with you
Comes from the mountain of light
I bring to you tonight.

Lying With You

Creek beds flowing
Through the earth
Golden grasses
Embrace my womb
With gentle caressing
I welcome you as the divine breeze
Enters me.

I AM Here to BE

He:
I must be perfect
For I am
Flawed inside
I run
When you see me
Dying inside
Love me
Or leave you
I will not die to my pride
Please do not see
The mirror I have
To me
What will I do
If the light comes through
Will it crack?
When it does
Will I lose
Everything
That I have?
Understand
I can walk away
I do not need you
The me inside
Is not ready
To come out
To not hide
It cannot meet
My perceived expectations
Of who I need to BE

For you
How can I make
You happy when
The lock to my heart
Is rusted and broken
Love me for who I am
Shattered
And just a token
Of the wealth
I am here to BE.

She:
I am the morning dove
Calling you
Through the wind
Let down the curtain
Feel the spin
Go through its center
Feel the knock on the door
I know you can't handle anymore
It's time, you see
That to BE
Who you want to BE
Means
Cracking apart
The glue
You created
Holding together
The tears and the pain
Inside the wound
Is a love
So deep
It will rock you

Gently to the beat of God's heart
That I am silently
Singing for You.
I AM here to BE.

How You See Your Self

I forgive myself
For needing you
To BE
The love that I see you to BE
As you come into your Self
To feel like a success
I don't want to be used to support your game
Pretending
You are fine
While in the design
Of your mind
There exists a way
Of BEing
Refusing to love and touch
The light of truth
Living inside
How you see your Self.

One Pearl

I remember you from an ancient design
Cast as one pearl
Sterling notes written forever
Lover's passion never ceasing
Open handed
Your heart reaches into mine.

Play in Our Love

After the embers died
A new flame rose up
From your desire to BE
More than the mask
You have worn
My love for you
Has held your heart
Even when you were
Too afraid to stay
In the heat
You are not alone
The leopard, panther and cobra
Become you
When you step away
From the chains of fear
Holding you
Powerless
Cast in shame
Along time ago
When no one knew
But you
The greatest gift
You have given me
Is saying yes
To the longing
In your heart
To choose your Self
Instead of the imposter
Who thought you were helpless
And worthless

A star of light
Who kept the shine
Of his divine gift
Hidden
Lie upon these orange rose petals
Play in our love
Gently stroke my body
Until I become One
With the undulations
Of our passion
Cast in honey and gold
I melt
Surrendered to your touch
I have waited
To be loved
As only you
Know how to love.

All Night Long

The willow tree
Leans down to the earth
To remember who she is
A nest from above
Wraps her love
Around me
I give myself
To the space
Between my body
And the song
Of the wind
That calls me home
To you
I have waited my whole
Life to find you
Here in the womb within
The home I find in your arms
For you have become
My willow tree
Holding me
All night long.

Hold Me Close

You touched the golden goodness
Neglected through time and space
Loved beyond measure
I treasure your grace
Your countenance of love
Streaming on the wings of the dove
Beckons me to come nearer
Closer to the source
Of your love
Forever touching life
Giving life I know
I am your creator
Playing in the fields
Of your luster
I paint my world
With your gaze
Weaving endlessly
The ribbons of your love
My love for you
Gently unites the rays
Of your eternal
Smile and Embrace.

Inside the Garden

All that I have lost
By leaving myself
Behind
I will commit to gather my soul petals and flames
To shine through me
I understand my pain is the same
As the world's wound
Grown in magnitude from leaving what is real
Inside the garden
Of our love.

Beyond Survival

My grandfather used sex to control
His uncontrollable passions and desires
To tame the inner voice
Shouting to have more
And conquer his fear of being human and hungry

My grandmother used sex
To make everything right
To please and make better
The pain of her man
That she felt responsible for eliminating

She thought her vagina was a vessel
For her man's release of his denied power
To truly love
She wanted him to love himself more
So she would open her legs
To give him
A place to embed his need to survive
While shitting down the voice
Of his true survival
The song of his own heart

As I come back to my Self
I realize
The song has become louder
My desire to love has become stronger

The desire to see you free
Consumes me
The pain we once brought to one another is melting
As we allow ourselves
To be held
For BEing exactly who we are

As expressions of the light and dark
Reuniting
From bondage into love
I find me
So I can see me
I love me
So I can give
You my essence
Hold me in your heart
Embrace the world through my heart
BE with me
BE with you
Embrace
The world in love.

Latch Undone

My mind now knows
How my heart loves you so
My heart no longer questions
My mind refuses to go
To where it has been comfortable before
It can no longer slumber at the door
It holds open the gate
So that you may enter
I keep the latch undone
So that the wind of your love
Can blow through
I lie down at your feet
I hold them close to my heart
And kiss them as we meet
Separation is gone
I feel no remorse
For what may or may not have happened
My past
You have always been here
In love
We will meet.

The Shiver

Heavens invitation
To end this cruel
Smorgasbord of pain
Close the curtains
She says
Let's undress
Under the covers
So no one including me
Can see
The shiver
Of my soul
As you climb inside of me.

Stop when I want
She screams
Take your time
He whispers
Can you see
The lights are off
The price we pay
For living in stone
Caught being cast alone.

Waiting to come
So we can
Roll over
And be done
Sprinkling breadcrumbs
Before the sun rises.

The Split

Good girl
Bad girl

Black pearl
White pearl

Open door
Closed door

Angry boy
Non-confronting boy

Live your life
Kill your life

Hot
Cold

Bold
Told
Your secrets are melting
In the light

Fight
Sight

Forward
Backward

Empty
Full

Frozen
Boiling

Maddening
Aloof

Blame Shame
End of game

Lame
Tame
All the same

Haunt
Bought

Women on their knees
For you

Stoic orgasms
No promises given

If I love you
How you want

Makes me feel better
About who I cannot be

Rather be this
Than to be hit and miss

And have to face
Pain and misery

I can't look at myself
Neither can you

We will kill each others heart
With the crime
Of forgetting
The way
Of love
Without consulting
The divine.

Set Him Free

The feminine dark power
Can walk a fine line
As she explores her power
She can play one person against another
She can touch a man's wound
Receiving all that he is
The man does as he should
Becomes what she wants him to be
She must set him free
Instead of being an illusion
Deterring his way home
She must be willing to see the seduction
Rising his fire so that she is all he desires
What does pure love look like
A heart wide open
Serves the reflection
To BE the light
Of her soul
Gives the man
Back the key
To die
Into love
To set him Self free.

Moving Forward

All by myself
I have wearied
Along this long journey
Help me
I scream
Let me out of this dream
Laughing at my needs
You are stuck
In not knowing how
Love really works
You cannot provide
You sit passive hiding
By my side
Letting me do everything
Yet you are a king
Who has forgotten to sing
My thirst for life
Cannot be quenched
Until you rise up
To confront
Patriarchal demands
Commanding your soul
To ignite what is bold and true
Without shame
You must do this for me
I cannot carry this load alone
Now is the time
I see you
Show up for me
Merge with the old

And continue
Forward in the new
Hold my hand
Kiss my lips
Let me know
You are here
To the end.

Together

Distant moons
Between your heart and mine
Prevent our dreams from merging
Long cords holding us
Beyond space and time
Together
My mind
Melts into streams
Of gushing desire
I remember me
When we are One
I remember us
When we are apart
Together we
Dance
Throughout eternity
Waiting to go
Home together.

To the Sea

Drop by drop
Liquid gold
Melts my flesh
Returning me to the sea
Becoming salt
I merge into your mouth.

Resurrect

Yesterday I turned away from the noise
And rose up from the grave
Leaving behind the bitterness
Of you burying your pain.

Transparent

Each step disappears beneath my feet
Taking me closer to you.

Held

I want to run
Into your love
Instead you carry me.

Nothing But You

Clarity reveals the joy
Of nothing
But You.

Invitation

I practice playing the scales of harmony
You run your hands
Through my spine
Inviting me to speak.

Golden Goblets

Liquid love
Pours through me
Casting pearls into the sea
Golden goblets
Filled in joy
Tumbling starlight
Through your eyes
Come rushing forth
To BE with me
BE with me.

Birthing

Dark embraces Light
Light embraces Dark

Dark supports Light
Light supports Dark

Swirling mists
Create energy
In motion
Into the night

One with the dance of molecules
Our bodies
Breathe life into their nucleus
Sustained by the transmutation of the unknown

The void
In its darkness
Is the womb
For the light
To BE born

Alas, God is birthing itself
Through our bodies
Igniting
The union of masculine and feminine aliveness

Pulsating through the veins of God
In sexual Oneness
Rays of light undulate

Expanding
Birthing
Color filaments
Connecting
Sustaining all life
In its web

Enlighten
Into the creator
Breathe
Its sweet nothingness
Drink this eternal nectar
Feel it
With me now.
Anticipation

We enter
The moist dunes
Of the ocean
Where the tide
Ebbs and flows
Into the cave
Where shadows
Have subsided
And golden
Droplets
From the ancient
Portal above
Pours its blessings
Into our anticipation
And dreams
Of union

To melt
Into the water
Of eternity
Keeping our embrace
Sacred
We merge
Into our sea
Of bliss.

Come With Me

Each gaze
Each sigh
Each inhale
Each exhale
Each waiting
Moment
For the serpent
To arise
You raise me
You bring me
Closer to my source
And as I enter its temple
I bring you with me
Into its chamber
Beyond the known
Into love beyond fear.

Freedom

One song
One pulse
One liquid sigh
You wait
I come
I wait
You come
Only the beginning
We flow
Into the heartbeat
Of the universe
The eternal darkness
Beyond our mind
Into light.

The Dance

I am quenched
By the spiral
Forever
Moving through me
Its orchestra
Tuning my channel
Of infinite light
I merge into its
Invitation
To BE One with
Its song
The lyrics
Sustain as color
Humming in harmonic
Oneness
Only birds could fly
Upon the currents
Created by the Oneness
Of your smile.

The Awakening

The grass feels its way to pasture
Crystalline structures covered in dew
Cells swelling in capacity
Melting lines
Void separating form
Without form
Hearts casted in new life
Melting, joining, returning, blending, defining
Hues of creation
Night beckoning day
Awakening tremors
Paths in to the center
Where fire lives and dragons breathe
Flying open
Portals of life
Waiting
No longer alone
Yearning beckons
Will igniting willingness
Refusing death
Patterns marking lighted streets
Born from the shadows
Black and white exposure
Symbols on paper
Burning magnified dust
Clay fired
Glazing boundaries
The urn pours it cream
Berries coat tongues
Ravishing in delight

The bed sheets are cool
Skin against skin
The heat off your back
Embraces our world
Awakening what is real.

In Love

Infinite heart
Speaking to the One
Drawing you near
Seeing fear
Disappear
Patience
Compassion
Longing to BE
In love
With me.

Spirit's Flame

Two flowers, two mountains, two streams
One moon, One sun
One beginning, One ending
The wind is silent as the word speaks
Through the faith of One Heart
Blossoming In Spirit's flame
On this Spring eve
The power of creation, rebirth, new vision rests
In the cradle of truth
One heart, One love, One eye, One voice
I celebrate all life
The laughter
Of our hearts BEing beckoned home
Into the ecstasy of Light's passion and embrace
The smile of God's power exploding
Our limitations in a twinkle
The return to the throne
To the kingdom
Of blessings
For the union of Oneness
Enlightens our way
Loving
The Allness
Lit
Blazing tenderness
From God's chamber to our chamber
The nectar
Divining the way
The succulence of all passion at our feet
Praises to the One

From One heart to One heart
Opening to remembrance
Lifting and embracing the seed
In perfect union
Restoring life's creation
A new blueprint
For all.

Walk Through the Door

He jumps off the rim
Ready to swim
Filled to the brim
He rambles and rolls
To embrace his new power
His life has paid the toll
And instead of jumping out of the tower
He decides to get out of the shower
Of continous tears
He thanks all who have served him
As he walks through the door
Ready to hear his soul roar
He is done seeking more
The fibers tore
And now mending
He is sending
Gratitude to the universe
For blending his mind, heart and soul
To come knocking on his door
His hand on the doorknob
Ready to turn
He lets go of blame
And gives back the shame
Realizing there is nothing left to gain
His heart seeks the new
The beautiful
Like a free sail at sea
He calls a new woman
Someone shining to be
The radiant anchor and lover

To create a new start
Young and vibrant, surrendered and whole
Peaceful and magnetic
Untettered and free.

Shamelessly

She cannot feel
She cannot see
Her tide rises and flirts
Shamelessly
She cannot see
She does not know
How the sea remembers
Her name
Eternally
Each wave feels no pain
She exclaims
I want to be like you
Rolling free
Make me like thee
The sea roars
Dissolve your Self
As salt immersed in water
Playing the flute with no breath
Liquefy all contrasts
Separating you from me
And me from thee
BE free of separation
Together
BE free.

Source of Grace

Wrap your body around the center
Of your unrequited love
Drop the boundaries of desire
Throw your Self into the fire
See the wisdom of your perfection
Before you seek another round
Receive the grace of perfect understanding
The miracle of love
Drop your mind into the garden
Of infinite returns
BE the social light of acceptance
Love your neighbor fully blessed
Seek the body of soul's pure desire
Releasing pain into the sea
Drive the cruelty of deception
Into stars of blazing faith
Wrap your arms around your love
Wrap your arms around your pain
Wrap your arms around your judgment
Wrap your heart around life's gift to BE
Exactly true to you
Wrap your arms around the lover
Waiting to BE born
Wrap your silence
Around the song
Exhaling out its wholeness
Exuding its sweat and tears
Ready to BE freed
Wrap your arms around the box
You have created for your Self

Cracks, imperfections, holes, and fears
Letting God destroy the rest
Drive your heart with total commitment
Follow passion as your guide
Unsettling the hardened sediment
Of your dislocated lies
Wrap your body around your heart
Your heart around your body
Embrace the servants all around you
Who have signed up to set your free
Wrap your arms around the darkness
Feel what you can birth
Wrap your soul around the light
See
To BE free
Give the source of Grace
Within you
The space to guide the way
Lie down beside the river
Let your fears float away
Wrap your arms around the freedom
Of forgiveness
Through the pain you perceive
Refuse the shame that keeps you bound
Destroy the myth of unholiness
Receive the release of convicted sin
Fan the fire
As it burns your judgment
Into ashes of severed love
Embrace eternal madness
Give no name to what keeps
You bound in iron chains
Melt through the resistance
Of self-created hatred

By embracing who you are
Wrap your arms around the freedom
Stop selling your life away
Come into my arms my love
May the song of souls union
Be allowed to BE told
Inviting presence of your purpose
To exhale and BE the guest
To stay to live unraveled
The trust held within you
Giving you a face
Into bridges of connection
New directions that set you Free
To BE
A new power of creation
Opening you to see the we
The holy trinity of remembrance
You belong to thee
Return to bliss
Open for the kiss
God's light has never forgotten
The lamp you hold
That can never be sold
Stand at the mountain ridge
Feel heaven as your bridge
Fly where wings cannot take you
Where only light
Rises behind the crevice
Of superficial lies
Breaking all ties
That bind you to thinking love is given
When it has never been taken away.

The Moon of Your Light

Descending Into Honey
Precious lover hold me close
End your mind
Wanderings
As the clouds
Part revealing
The moon
Of your light
End your sorrows
Fall in love
As the wind captures
Your dreams
With love
Descending
Into the honey
God has created
For you to eat
Rise up with your song
Open the petals of your heart
As you caress the lips
Of creation
Here is your new vocation
BE One in your heart
Walk through the door of your soul
May your passion BE bold
May every story BE told
As you wrap your heart
Into Gold
Where darkness meets the light

Making love to the silence
All identities crumbling
As the universe
Merges into the night.

Melting Her Mind

She laughs as the wind
Dances through her body
For the first time
Her body carries
The magic of her heart
Into her senses
Mindfully awakening
Her breath
Quickens to ride
The wave of life
Carrying her pelvis
To the rhythm
Of her soul
Melting her mind
Into its ecstasy.
She roars.

Sun and Moon

We
Pull back the curtain
Surrounding
Our sacred bed
Throwing fresh rose petals
Onto its sheets
We look
Into each others eyes
Holding steady
The bond of trust
We have lovingly created
Undressing one another
Slowly at first
We ignite the golden radiance
In our bodies
Shining through the window
Of life
Sun and moon
Ignite this moment
Circle around one another
Naked awareness in love.

Into the Heart of Love

Deep within the universe
Rests the sanctuary
Of life
Ocean, meadow, creek
Pour
To meet the awaiting
Volcanic eruption
Blessing the land
With its steady
Torch of fire
Growing in my womb
Yearning and desire
Emerge into life
As the power of creation
Groans
In the sea of bliss
We are newborns
Evolving into the waves
Of ecstasy
Together
We
Become One
In the knowingness
That our sacred nakedness
Reveals the sexual kiss
Of ten thousand seeds
Exploding as moans
Of rebirth

The heart of love
Breaks through
Awakens.

Meld As One

Colors ride
Upon currents
Of fire
Bursting in promise
Of ignition
Cognition
Recognition
Of the eternal
Light that you are
Saturating waters
Soaking through your skin
Letting in
The breath of life
The sound
From deep within
As earth and sky
Meld as One
Connect you
In peace
The tree divine
Up your spine
Rattles snowflakes
Upon the heat
Of self reflection
Self deception
Ending thoughts
Of condemnation
Throwing them into the fire
Of lost desire

Enter the shelter
Into the fur
Of my warmth
Roll into my belly
Making love again.

Fully Here

You are born competent
To BE your Self
Upon your heart
Is placed the wound
Of self deceit
By others
Who have torn
Apart their own sacred
Trust with Creator God
Instead they stab
The innocent
Who become afraid
That they are somehow damaged
No longer held valuable
Treasured and seen
As the competence
That they are
To love, serve, and resurrect
The dying and neglected
Dreams and visions
Held within
When Self condemnation
Take the place
Of Self competence
Thoughts and fears
Of yester years
Grow as we come
Closer to cracking
Through our cocoon
Fully here

You are held
In your wetness
And sweat
As fear
Dissolves
Into the love
That makes you real
Melding gold
Into competence
Condemnation no longer
Allows
Love to infiltrate
Your heart, your soul
Every cell within you
When self-doubt erupts
Enter the kingdom
Of light
That waits within your heart
Awaken your genitals with love
Soothe them instead
Of abusing them
Receive their red fire
Their burning desire
To merge with God
Uniting Oneness
Within your heart.

Empty Your Chalice

Create your moments
To BE beautiful
Shine with the stars
Glide with the tides
Grow as the seedling
BE in the heartbeat
Of the tree that you are
Know your branches and leaves
Spread to the sky
Roots of power
To the earth
Stand in the center
Where you can fly and dive
Into the heart of
Love
Empty your chalice
So we can enter
The palace
Of rubies and gold.

Open Your Petals

Respond as the rose
Turn your face
Towards the rain
To receive cleansing
Rays to clear
Humanity's pain
Your ability
To open your petals
And see through
A hundred eyes
Are One
With the sunflower
Seeds
Contained in the nucleus
Of the sun
Preparing to shed
Their seeds
Into the bowl
Of summer ripening
Into sweet fruits.

Raising Mist

Perfect
Listening
BEing and receiving
Penetrate love
From within the heart
Of light
The galaxy of motion
An open doorway
To the presence
Of BEing One
With the diamond
Of wisdom
Saturating
Your soul
With the fire
Raising
Mist
The earth
Transforms
Doubt into trust
Passion returning
Raindrops
Into reflection
Beyond sight.

In the Wind

You came to me
Naked as a leaf
Free of its attachments
To the tree
It was born to grace
I will miss
Your sweet greenness
As you invite me
To roll over and around you
Until I am covered
In your petals
BEing spread
By the desire
To reach the wind
And BE carried away
Into the starry night
That is enraptured
By every planet spinning
Its song
As I sing your praises
To Venus
Orchestrating the clouds
To reveal
Pure darkness where love
Turns into passion
Resting its breasts
Into your heart
Etching the crest

Of eternal light
We begin where each breath
Swells and ends.

In Our Hearts

Liquid gold
Spreads its wings
Transparent veils
Reveals the earth
Pulsating through
Our hearts
As we reduce
Time into unlimited space
And face
The sorrows we have left
Rest as pebbles
On the river bed floor
Currents
Of light
Begin to lift us
Into the home
We have seeded
For eons of time
Now gently smiling
They bud
Their glorious
Scent of arrival
In our hearts
Ready
To birth
Their wildness
Beckoning us
To let go
Beyond memory
Where water meets

The earth
In cosmic desire
One with the fire.

In Love

Released in the wind
The river
Grabs her heart
And returns her
To the moss
Covered currents
Flowing from the cave
Of no desire
Entering the shrine
Of darkness
She pulls herself
Close to the cool earth
Feeling the water flowing over her body
She enters
The pure light
Of the eternal sun
Released by the fire
Of her passion
To know bliss
She balances remembrance
With surrender
And kisses the droplets
Of nectar swimming
To meet her empty mind
In love.

Ready To Melt

Tender glances
Here we are
Meeting again
A long ago promise
To walk
Into the sun
Together
Facing east
I see eternity
Spread as the wings
Of my heart
I cannot stop
Loving you
Aching
I am pulled
Towards you
Ready to melt
As One
Into the One.

I Have Always Loved You

There is a song
Sung in silence
Beyond the call
Of the wild
Heart
Sitting alone
In my cave
Free in the light
I invite you
To join me
In my home
Of transparency
And delight
Beyond motion
Embraced in creation
I come to you
Again.

Diamonds of Love

She captured
The river
As it glided
Through her body
Turning red rock
Into rubies
Emeralds into hearts
The earth
Became alive
As she wrapped
Her legs around
The diamonds
Within your heart
Turning gravel
Into dust
Longing into fulfillment
The mountain
Rose to meet
The joy
Beyond all pain
And desire
Rising from one glance
To meet
In love
Once again.

Climb the Branches

Purposeful intention
Can't always get
You to the top of the mountain
Surrender
How you get there
Align your mind to the Spirit
Within your soul
Reunite the light and dark
Let go into the trembling
Volcanic passion
Rising
In your spine
Let the sun ignite
The moon of your eye
With delight
Give me your sorrows
Climb the branches
Of my love
To the sky.

Melt

Each moment
We touch each other's heart
Reaching into the darkness
Of creation
I am spellbound
By the kiss
Of your soul's touch
The blood of your wound
Is returned to the earth
Growing meadows of wild flowers
The leap of your stride
Captures eagles
Spell bound
As they dance
Through the crest
Written upon your chest
Leaving behind
Celestial melodies
Of meeting death in its face
Rebounding through the birth
That marks your name
Inscribed upon the tree
Of life
Lift your face to the sun
Dissolve into me.

Ashes

When the wind blows
The sound of your hoofs
Touch the sky
As thunder
Rolls through our bodies
And light touches
The soles of our feet
Igniting our hearts
To remember
The melody
Of wonder and pure delight
I bring ashes
Of longing
To the fire
Of our love.

The Story

Each breath carves through
The story
Told through fear
Each exhale
Releases the tears
Held by memories
Witnessed by the moon
Dissolving time into presence
Love is mirrored back
Everywhere
The ripples of the lake
Reflect the storm
Breaking through
The muscles of resistance
I hold you in my arms
As you weep
In gratitude
For the life
You have been given
We return to the beginning
Where together
The story
Of love
Emerges from the earth
As One.

I Am the Rain

Beyond your shame
Comes the rain
Of love
Seeping into the earth
Of joy
Where light
Ignites
The source
Of comfort
Found only
Through remembering me
By remembering you.

Ride the Wave

Inside the shell
Of disgrace
Lies the shame
Of the human race
Standing in the water
The tides are rising
What will I choose to do
The longing
Continues
To ride the wave
Of love
Take me higher
Into the fire
Where I no longer exist
In your kiss
Tender is your pain
That melts
Into the foam
As we are taken into bliss
Carried beyond desire
We bring heaven
On to earth
With each breath.

Song of the Rose

Its time to go to bed
This is what she said
The day dissolved
The night evolved
The mist around the moon
Cleared
As the melody
Of love drew near
I wrap my body around you
To celebrate your heart
I climb on to you
Creating a new start
Where love never ends
As we build BEing friends
Humbled to honor
The ability to merge
The heart
Requires nothing
But presence and grace
I bow to your soul
Celebrate the light that you are
Sing the song of the rose
Permeate the night
Melting into light.

From Darkness Into Light

Guide me into your passion
Of the night
I return the doubts
And questions
Brought
From lacking sight
The cry within my heart
Now releases terror
Through the heat
As we become One
Descending
From the
Sun
BEing
Rebirthed
Through
Transmutation
Golden glow of truth
Resurrecting
From darkness
Into light.

Where Will I Find You

Everywhere I have looked
For you
Wrapped by you
Losing my Self
In you
When I found you
A part of you
Was owned
By others
Who kept
Your heart
For themselves
Even though you
Did not know
The sorrow that you
Carried
Was all that you had
To bring you through
The darkness deep within
Where comfort
Was confused as love
Control taken for security
Unhealed yearning for
A mothers touch
Could mend your broken wings
Chained to the earth
By womens caresses
Who could own you
Without having to save you

Your sexual energies
Fed their need to have more
Power than what they could
Store and be sure
Their souls had a place
To reside
Inside of the man
That could not be
Trained to walk
Without pride
For what he gives from inside
Thinking he was making a difference
Yet fell into the hell
Of his making
Refusing to end finding
Connection to himself
Through the dark
Of loneliness
Will you
Learn how to see
For your Self
Through the eyes
Of the warrior leopard
How you give others
The secret weapon
To take everything that you have
And leave you
Impoverished
To depend upon
Them to feed you
The life force that you give
To others
Hopefully giving
Meaning to life

That you decided
Was cruel
You stripped your Self
Worthless
Alone in the rain
Now sitting in the desert
The split cedar trees
Wait for waters
From winter rains
BE held my love
By the healing grief
Waiting for you
In the dried tears
Of your loss
Fill the bucket
From within you
Let the sun
Shine once again.

Touching Home

She laughed
As she let go
Of her fear
Of BEing too much
And decided to jump
On the back
Of her favorite dragon
That she had kept
In the closet
Of her heart
Bound to direct the orchestra
Of her life
She discovered her power
Was gentle
And strong
Having nothing to prove
Resist or defend
She danced
By the sea
With the wind at her back
Feeling One with waves
Releasing her heart
To BE
Once again.

Finding The River Again

The river took her in its heart
Peeling off her bark
Crickets sang to remind her
To trust the hands of love
Undone returned to wetness
Undulations rang through her body
As cobwebs of time
Stirred her into shifting course
Finding the river again
Gave her purpose
To enter the rhythms of ecstasy
Until she had become One
With the sun
Shedding her skin
The song of her bones
Danced with the fire
Of the moon
Pulsating up her spine
She entered the bliss
Of your kiss.

Waves of Joy

She loved until the moon came up
Until her soul caught fire
Through the cosmic flame
Her body drenched in rose water
His light delivered her passion
Into waves of joy
She came to him
Renouncing all fear
Until the moon dipped down upon the horizon
Melting the beads of divine light
From his brow
The silence of their love
Kissed the night.

One Gaze

Through the glass door
The dream of separation shattered
Into the tigers eye
Burning into ash
Footprints step
Into time
Leaving behind
The life we had lived
Rain comes
Cascading
Down your back
I climbed the tree
And raised the earth
Beyond
The sun
We felt the stillness of creation
Dark and deep
Where my heart no longer beats
On its own
It pulsates
To your touch
Arching my longing
Around your tongue
One gaze
One heart
Soaring on freedoms belly
The tiger rips me open
To your love.

Free Fall

In and out of time
Exhausting patterns
Until we release
Into the center
Where the One verse
Of reason
Becomes extinct
Through contraction
The mind
Releases
Its grip
Beyond its Self
We expand
Where nothing is held
Feared or kept
A secret
We free fall
Into love
Cascading through space
The waterfall
Of fulfillment
Holds us
As we merge
Into droplets
Of infinite bliss
One source
One heart
One flame.

Until You Yearn

Until you yearn
For my kiss
You will never understand
What it feels like to lie
Beside you all night long
Waiting
For you to feel my heart
Aching to love
Until you yearn
For Gods kiss
You will never understand
What it feels like
As God
To wait for you
To turn to Him
Opening the door
She reveals the veils
To be kissed
Into freedom
When you let go
And surrender
The anxiety
You keep
To remind you
That love hurts
Your life is not yours
And you have no right
To be in your body
For the sake of your own joy

For you belonged
To a sexual tyrant
Who kept the key
To your erection
The pleasure was his
Until you yearn
To know
Love
Beyond what your mind
Is able to grasp
I will remain outside
Your window
Waiting for you to see
The sun rising
Next to me.

Currents of Our Love

Magic dancers by the sea
Swell and open
For me to see
Glaciers melting in the rain
Fingers locked in golden mane
I am flying on this rapture
Unafraid now to be captured
Hold me down
Spread me wide
Grounded in the sounds
Of love
I AM
Mountains soaring
Freed to ride
Blue currents of our love.

Able To Sleep

Sometimes the heart can crack
While waiting
For one's lover
To wake up
From a deep sleep
Of justifying their right
To play with your heart
While pretending that because
They left their own heart
For matters more important
Their mind
Now held frozen in time
Refuses to stay
With the orgasm
They had
Even though it blew
Their mind
They push aside their heart
To be opened and closed
At will
As I fall over the rocks
On our path
The bones of the hand
In which I have given
Everything I have to you
Fractures
Now the pain must reset
My heart
As my feet
Pound the earth

With the sweat
Of anger
Wishing you had been
There a hundred times
Before
For me
Even though you
Believe you couldn't
And turned your back
Your eyes
Your thoughts
Far away into problems
You made yours
To escape your feelings

I reached out to an empty
Shell wishing you were mine
Only you can tell your Ego
Its time here is complete
Perhaps only then
I will BE
Able to sleep.

The Eyes of My Beloved

The wind returns
Through the space between my leaves
I leave my hut
To find you home alone
I whisper can you see me
But you have gone away
Into the misty winter of long yesterdays
Can I find you and bring you home my love
Can I send you messages on the wings of doves
To give you what I know how to give the most
The door to my heart opens to you
Waiting in the stillness of the dawn
The eyes of my beloved
Returning for me
Waiting to set me free
I walk slowly into the arms of love
Leaving my life behind
As I knew it
Freed forever.

To BE

After the world of love opened
I found the freedom to receive
Your love and BE in the infinite
Wellspring of love
As the power generator
I was born to BE.

All That I Can BE

I penetrate my heart to meet myself
Without a doubt I come to me
So that I can see what is real and true
For me to BE when I step into your arms
All that I can BE.

Through the Night

She climbs into the rose
Spreading her toes
Into its soft petals
Its scent enters her body
Her breath permeates
The hairs of her nose
As she lifts into the seventh sense
Beyond time
Laughing within a new design
Courage transforms into presence
Presence into wonder
Wonder into thunder
As the rain falls
The roof sings
In rhythm with the yearning
Of her heart
The story of union
Is told through their kisses
As lightning consummates their love
Through the night.

Into Remembrance

Pouring nectar
Through the branches of my tree
The sap holds your love
In my heart
In the center of my BEing
I remember your touch
As snowflakes dance upon my face
Your touch inside the bark
Of my old self
Strips away the skins of protection
That come
When I doubt the love
That is my birth song
The presence of creation
You gently rock me
I sway in your melody
Enter me and take me to your kingdom
Raising me once again
Into remembrance we meet
Embracing
Our bliss.

Melt Into Love

Your heartbeat is your ally
Your sexuality your friend
A hidden language of communication
That never has an end
Open the door
To the pain you have endured
Take the plunge into the river
Draw my body near
Take me as yours
Melt into love
Remember
The sorrows you have
Been given
Were only meant
To remind you
Of the falsities
You have believed
Needed to be endured
Cast aside the coat that you were given
Crack open your false mind
As the enemy
That keeps you from Love
You cannot get or take what you do not
Already have
Find what you hate inside
Open up the gate
Find the light within your heart
Pour its cosmic love
Upon the scars
Become the sea

Dissolve as salt
Ride the wave
Find the dream
Of your beloved
Ready to be seen
Born to feel
Drench your senses
In the beauty
Of God's eternal dream
Step through the portal
Find the lover in your soul
Take the risk of BEING
Feel the universe
Beating in your chest
Divine mother
Beneath your feet
Dancing you to surrender
Divine father
Giving laser light
Where only you and love remain
One unto your Self
Let go of your game
Release the shame
Used to blame
There is nothing left to gain
Take my rose
Into your heart
Fly free
On the wings of the dove
BE free
My love.
.

Power of Love

When she walks on water
The sky opens
To receive her passion
For the music played
During our kisses
Keeps me up all night long
How can one soul
Ignite
Another
When the beauty of God
Beholds the container
Of love
Nothing can stop the music
Only the power
Of creation
Can fuel our life
Into motion
Returning us
To our original
Birth
Where eternity
Plays it notes
Into one melody
Where only God exists
As the power of love.

Ladder To the Sky

Mountain pattern
Sky hued design
Shadowed windows
Frosting in air
Comfort given
As stars fill the night
Patient caring
Without being overbearing
Sacred light
Shining in the meadow
Rivers streaming
Through my mind
Be kind she whispered
As she disappeared into
The fog
Lifting
Tender sweetness
I roll onto your chest
Dissolving into your heart
Quickening my soul
As elk hoofs pound across the earth
My body pulses in love
Strengthening eternal presence
As I am drawn into the core
Of creation
I ride the horse
Into intoxication
Bliss opening
Undulation
Exhaltation

Nostrils flaring
Unbarring
The ladder to the sky.

Communion

The quarter moon
Becomes
My back arching
To the sky
Cobra releasing
Love into seven heads of light
As golden rays
The divine
Lifts us higher into cosmic
Roots of impassioned desire
Transpires into melodies
Of ecstasy
Gathers you up
Inside of me
Holds you
As the flower finding peace
Welcomes the bee
Open laughter
In our union
Brings our souls
Into communion
Rose anointed kisses
Coming into love
Holds us in
Recognition
Of the One
Source of freedom
Releasing us into flight
Earth wings
Felt as home

One eye in delight
Soaring into stillness
Beyond time and space
The stars have found us tonight.

Upon the Wave

I wait
Until the Milky Way
Spreads its foam
Into the ocean of this night
I wait
For your love
Shining the lantern
Of a thousand years
Through the jewels
Of my soul
The pounding of the surf
Enraptures the smooth
Silky breath of the tides
Meeting me when I least expect
It to BE
Everything needed
To guide me home
Into the ebb and flow
Of the rhythm
Of your heart
I am carried
Upon the wave
Of ecstasy
To you.

In Your Love

Open me slowly
When the hurt
From your words
Touches into my soul
Penetrating my boundaries
Makes me succumb
To your control
Give me time
To hold my own
Standing in my love
I give to myself
The love
I need
To open to you
With ease
And natural grace
Let me be
At my pace
When you know
My heart
Has been hurt
I will open
As the morning glory
Greets the sun
To the love
That you are
To the love
That you give
To the One
I adore

And yearn
To explore
All
The ways
Your love
Caresses
Enters me
Stay in me
So I can merge
In your love.

In Mother's Love

When she enters you
Everything stops
But the movement
Of love
Can you feel her
As she wraps
Her arms
Around you
And draws you
Into her eternal
Song
Where roses and gardenias
Surround you in life
Ignite
Make your orgasm
Last all day
Treasure your body
Open your mind
Free your fear
Tell your lover
By the way you
Hold him
To receive
Through the night
Set your flame on fire
Fulfill your desire
Make love your mantra
Know Divine Mother
Within your heart.

Why Wait

Climb my vine
Drink the wine
I have made for you
Come into the womb
Where stars and meteors meet
Into the spinning vortex
Where love
Explodes the galaxy
Of my heart
Why wait
When the door
Has already been opened
To the petals
Giving life to your fire.

I Kissed You

I kissed you in the fog
In the early morning
Light
As the trees stood
In stillness
Waiting for the breeze
I became the water
Of the sea
As it permeated
My heart
The cobra of your soul
Became One
With the pulse
Of our life blood
Beating as music
With divine
Cadence
The doors opened
To the hidden paradise
Of Earth's magic kingdom
BEing retold
To breathe.

After the Veil Is Lifted

Surrounding my heart
Are rose petals
Of divine nectar
Pulsing through
My veins
Giving
Life and care
To the wounded
And the hungry
In gratitude
You take my hand
To your lips
Yet the pain
In my roots
From watered
Down messages
Of love
Created by closing the door
When I least expected
Through pulling away
Blaming me for the pain
That has scarred
Your heart
My love wants to mend
The hurt
I yearn to be cared
For by your love
Waiting and praying
BEing and longing

For you to choose
Me
Over the pain
That grips you in the night
I am tired of this fight
The one you play out
In secret behind the bars
Of deep suffering
May your moans
Of pleasure
Set you free
To BE You in me
I welcome you
Home
To the power
That awaits you
While the veil is lifted.

When Love Grew

When she climbed
Through the notes
Of the music
She played
All was revealed to her
Heart
When she remembered
Why she came
Into the light of love
Her pelvis
Shook
Until
She entered
Into the mystery
Of wonder and passion
Joy filled her womb
As she received
The chord of fulfillment
Pulsing through
Her lovers veins
How could a kiss
Say so much
When love
Grew
Nothing was the same
The melody of longing
Became stronger
Until their voices
Were heard
Only by the thunder in the night.

As the Earth Rises

Our molten golden matrix
Fills the space
Between my heart and mind
Stripping the callous skin
That hides the rose
Within this heart
Naked awareness
Take me below the surface
Of your waves
Allow me to enter
As a breathless
Dolphin in joy
Naked awareness
Allow the water to penetrate
The membrane of remembrance
Within these cells of God
Calling me to dance in Oneness
As the earth rises
To enter my new skin
Revealed as velvet
Petals of a heart
That has yearned
To begin again without the shadow
Of others
Afraid of their naked awareness
The eyes opening in my body
Can see through your fear
And celebrate the You
That is near

As I touch you
And you touch me
The distance between us
Melts into the light
Of a thousand stars
Taking us into their arms
We are drenched in the sweat
Of love's passion
Naked awareness
Open the earth to enter my skin.

Bucket of No Regrets

She loved until the moon
Set and the ocean
Poured through the vessel
Of her love
Cyclones of desire
Cast their imprint
To meet the destiny
That tomorrow brings
Through the valley
Of the sea
She calls me
To my knees
As I drop the bucket
Of no regrets
Home in the tide
I dissolve my heart
Beyond
The limitations
I had perceived.
In my heart
Is returned
To the sea.

A New Constellation

She danced upon the wind
Until the sun
Came up
Igniting the mountain
In light
Joy entered our bodies
Until the container
Expanded into ecstasy
Without thought
Only feeling
Time stopped as
One breath
One heart
As you came into me
The stars became
A new constellation
Created by our desire
To create a new world
A pearl of passion
Circled us in
Power undulating
Eternity
Within my womb
New eyes to see
The magic of our union
Grows inside of me
Conceiving love
God has given
Through thee to me.

In Each Kiss

Climbing upon your thighs
My chest touching yours
The cobra enters my mouth
Filling me with intoxication
In every breath
Our heartbeat uniting in a new pulse
Hears the drum of the universe
As you lift me
To meet your mouth
Life surges
As it opens the door
For the nectar of God
To BE given
In each kiss
Eternity ripples
As time stands still
The story of re-creation
Told through undulation
Passion
Through my pelvis
Heart on fire
Nipples erect
As heaven and earth unite
Us
Anchoring love as the current
Beyond limitation
Where male and female power
Meet
I bow to your essence, your friendship, your grace
Adoring you

In surrender
I rise to meet you
As we find our pace
Receiving your nectar
Through the heart of my soul
My womb meets your power
With longing
With grace
As the light
Builds momentum
We become One
Where the ocean meets
The sublime
In love
Hands grasped
As ecstasy releases
Old ties
Ready to BE dissolved
Into the dark void
Igniting us
Within the universe
Where all
Is One
Once again.

Honor the Love

Walking
Through the terrain
Of reason, treason
Pain endured
Waiting for it to subside
Where there is no place to hide
I want you
To decide
What you want
Honor the love
That is felt
Inside the world
We create
There is no escape
From the fear
Until I hold it near
And raise it into God
To clear me of my mistakes
That keep me hostage
To wanting
You to take away my pain
Opening the gate
I come to my light
In surrender
Holding the truth
That I have always been
Enough
Living as the love
I have offered to you

We lie beneath
The stars
Of the night.

Until the Sun

The mountain birthed
Its message
Into her heart
As she felt his
Tenderness
Sweep away the fears
Created over millenniums
At last they have met up again
Facing his love
She melts
Into the sea of surrender
Never to be the same
Again
Has she become the love
Song that he plays
For her at night
Waiting for eternity to meet
Up again
As the mirror
Of illusion
Cracks
Nothing remains
But the ache of longing
In her heart
To roll in the grass
Of Oneness
With his eyes dancing
Between her thighs
Merging in the wind

That has the power
To dissolve their minds
Their bodies
The memories
Being captured in the smoke
Of prayers
Answered by the Mother's Grace
They lie in the waters
Of gold
Running their hands
Upon the curves
Of love
Until the sun
Penetrates their embrace
With compassion
For their innocence
Reflected back as prosperity
Given by the Ones
Who have watched them prepare
To receive the light
Upon their hearts.

Home To Me

Undulating curtains
Caress the window
Clearing
The future
As translucent waves
Ride
On golden wings
Painting a canvas
Created through
Being
In your arms
I call my destiny
Home to me.

Tears in the Mud

Resting in the ripples
Of your song
The water rushes to greet
My heart tonight
Longing has turned
Into patience
As the days dance
Forward through the flames
Of my heart
Once you felt so near
Now after so many
Moon rises
And feeling my empty bed
There is just a memory
Of you beside me
No longer able to wait
I weep my tears
Into the mud
Holding your footprint
In my heart.

Golden Resonance

Stillness
Holds open
The orchestral sounds
Lasting through the night
Of the last sustaining
Tone of this unquenched
Heart
Finding its golden
Resonance within the flowers
Of our heart
I surrender into each moment
Until our lips meet
Again in the light
Of the shiva moon.

When You Went Away

When you went away
My vagina had become One
With my heart
Closing with a prayer
I asked you to not leave
Too soon
The moon was rising
In my soul
Returning once again
The flame flickers
And finds it reflection
In the night sky
Oneness is tender
It takes time
To anchor its presence
Love was aborted
Life looks different
Through the eyes of One
Heart
You have brought
Me to earth
Through something
Newly created
That is not me
And not you
When you went away
Our newly created
Love that was growing
Into its own expression

Through the roots
Of my body
The vision
Of my mind
My soul expanding
Into us
When you went away
The life that was being created
To be born
Was too young
Too new
Too outrageous
Awakened in love
Without you
Half of the creation
Became dormant
Where do we begin
For what was created
Was destroyed
May Shiva come again.

Waiting For You

I became the moon
Tonight
As the current
Of love picked me
Up into the pulse
Of our hearts
Each cell in this body
Yearns for your touch
Lying next to you
The night is long
There is an ache
To love you
And to feel your kisses
To feel your legs wrapped around mine
Your lover waits to receive you
Thunder has already captured
My longing
Waiting for you.

This Silver Kiss

We miss one another
As the moon travels around
The sun of our love
Each beam from its silver
Kiss enraptures
And embraces
The longing to love you
Awake in the night
I wait for you
My lips on your back
Tonight
My love
Cannot hold back
Yet I feel us a million miles
Away
Life's logic cannot snuff out
The pulse
Of desire
Rising with the sun
Waiting to be
With you
Tonight
Your love shines to me
As the universe
Envelops us in its arms
What is in your heart
Each time you turn away
The morning seems further away
There is no way to leave
You

For I will not leave my
Self
Light has made us One
Your smile
The joy in your eyes
As we melt together
Tonight
I have dissolved
Into the honey
That awaits your kiss.

Salt

Drop by Drop
Liquid gold
Melts my flesh
Returning me to the sea
Becoming salt
I merge into your heart.

When Passion Strikes

I look in the inner
Mirror of my desire
And see you
Standing there
As God kisses
Your brow
Passion rolls
Through each breath
Yearning for you
Since you have returned
A magnet of love
Pulls me closer to you
Let the gate of divine
Reopen
Ecstacy in each kiss
Take me
To where you live.

In the Early Dawn

Winter windows
Dissolving morning rainbows
Into translucent moments
Of stillness
I wait your return
Tea leaves brewing
Waiting to sip
Frost into moonlit
Breath rising
Skin becoming energy
Light changing form
Awakening the sun
As darkness of creation
Becomes the cobra
Lifting up undulations
Into ecstasy
I move on to you
Until earth
Reverberates
My Being into stars
Pulsating the night
Into the rhythm
Of being born
Through our love
In the early dawn
Two hearts beat
Into BEing One.

Of Love

Sacred valley
Here in the creek
We meet in the caverns
Between the red rock
Of love
Eons of time
Merge through streams
Of love
Each time that I jump
Into the pool
Of love
You are waiting for me
To be blessed
In the eternal moment
Where there is no breath
Time stands still
As I exhale the moments
Of longing
For the love
That was wasted upon
Dry lips
Fleeting reunions
With only tastes of Oneness
Until I found you
In the meadow grasses
My true lion
Gazed at me
Finally remembering you
I wept in your arms.

I Give My Body to You

Your hands open the gates
Allowing love to enter
Mountains and valleys
Plateaus and mounds
You touch the ocean bed
Created from sands
Of smooth seaweeds
Moist and firm under your touch
I am sculpted into spirit
As I give my body to you
I have become molten lava
In your palms
I have become the sea
Translucent in your salt kisses
You have become the moon
As the tides of my body
Move with the rhythm
Of your firm deliberate
Touch dissolving my mind
To meet the invitation
Of becoming the woman
I AM
In the currents
Of the wave
I have yearned to ride
From the beginning of time
Infinite waves of love
I AM
Songs in ecstasy
Merge into one wave

My heart meets
Your touch
As we become One
I give myself to you.

I Turn To You

Whispering sands
Slowly moving through times
Funnel transposing windows
Shafts of light
Beckoning embrace
As the sun rises
Above the mountain
Stillness
I turn to you
Ready for the day
Of love.

In the Nest of Sweet Grass

Unpainted I see you
Transparent readiness
Enter the chamber
Where the mind must lie empty
In the nest of sweet grass
Your leaves
Tossed upon my head
Are turned into garlands
Protected from the storm
I offer songs
Of quiet joy
As you sleep untouched
Throughout the night.

Wild Nectar

Whistling leaves
Captured in the winds
Torrential currents
Wide opened destiny
Wings upon my soul
Torso and hips
Feet and head
Ride the thunderbolt
Of BEing alive
In your impulse
To love freely
From this golden heart
Wild nectar
Designed
In the image
Of expanded love
Infinitely knowing
Nothing will ever be the same.

Bark Of My Skin

Awakening windows
Where time forgets
Itself in silence
I enter
Your tunnel of wisdom
That calls me in gently
Remembering why
I came here
Your curiosity
Swells as luminescent
Domes of geological
Mysteries invite me
To rise in luster
Shining slick
Rain slides
As leaves of autumn
Contrasts golden orange
Imprints
Bringing
Truth
As my heart
Leaps into you
Leaving fear
In an attempt
To climb through
The bark of my skin
I strip back
All thoughts
So I can lie naked

In the drizzle
Of love
Remembering why
I came into your arms.

The Earth Within Me

Where has the world
Gone in its spin
Around the sun
Can I capture
Your shadow
Remove its tight coat
Can I bring
You warm water
To soak
Your weary feet
In the volcanic lava
Of melted dreams
Can I renew
Your thirsty spirit
Tired of aching
I lie awake
At night
Wondering why
You go and if you
Will return
Can I weave
Your broken heart
Into woven rays
Of music as heaven's rhythm
Enlighten your heavy load
Dance
May I lift you
Higher into my desire
Where light

Becomes the bed
To consummate
Lovers words
Etched into clouds
We release our burdens
As we fly
Into each others
Kisses
The earth within me
Is found.

Of Passion and Love

Swift currents merge
With the ongoing surging
Of love
Penetrating inside my chest
These breasts breakthrough
The confinements
Of love
Since life began
I have birthed you
Sheltered you
Welcoming you
Casts a shadow that has thrown
Even the strongest horse
Off its course
Why make believe
When the tidal wave
Of passion and love meet
At the door
Of spacious forgetfulness
To remember everything
You must forget everything
About you
So you can
Know me
Your Self.

Standing in Your Self

I climb the ropes that entangle your pain
I cut the ropes
To set free the toxins
Of self-hatred and remorse
Where is your sword
Why does your ego step up and take over
I do not
I will not
BE in relationship to the one who shoves the rest of you aside
This heart is weary
Your battle with the dark is now heavy in my womb
Captured in your maze I am confused and weak
My rage brews as you dart away from facing the split
When you say you are sorry
I forgive. I receive.
Hours or days later the pain hurts me again
When the holy light of God surrounds you
When will you fill your Self with its healing radiance
Will you turn to face your Self or continue to turn away from the hurt
The yearning of a child who does not know its own love waits to be loved by your love
The seeking eyes to feel joy clasps onto any perceived external wisdom source that is stronger than how it perceives it Self
This anger that I was blessed to take on was given to teach me what is precious
I value myself. I need you to value me.
Give your wounded child a voice so you can embrace his pain

Speak to my heart, take care of my heart, as you would take care of yours
Make the boundary with your child clear so you can honor mine
Keep the wave of love consistent
I want to ride the wave of our love
If I am let down it is only because you enter your inner world of confusion
Here hiding you ease the anxiety of your expectations to fix, make better, fulfill and resolve your problems that come from your internal mother and father, and pressure you to live in torment
We love. You love. I love.
Then, the broken poem of ecstasy, now fragments must be put back together again as you gain your equilibrium after you hide behind the frozen walls of your fear
Truly, you exist, yet who inside exists? There is only one You to love
He looks for rabbit homes in hard to find places and waits for the rabbit to entertain him before sunset.
Will you remember consistently the name written in your heart?
Source. I AM.
The mountain who upholds the sand upon the beach
The tribe of the wild four-leggeds gathering before the storm. I AM.
All of life lives inside of me. I AM.
From the hollow tree stump of decomposed roots
Your cup becomes empty
And I am left to fill it or run
If your cup is empty, I am abandoned
If you cup is full, we dance through the night in each other's arms

This anger. This rage. Comes from not knowing if you will abandon me or love me.
My source. I enter. I open to love. I open to your love
I am tested. Am I refused because of who I AM?
Yes. Its true.
Until you end your blaming that the truth I bring is a gift
Moments of deep union and love will be abandoned
Refusing to abandon myself brings me closer to me and further away from you
Do you expect me to just accept how you abandon your Self and consequently abandon me?
I am here to BE the love I AM.
To BE the love you seek, so you can find it on the inside
Unless you take down the walls to You, the anger simmering within you will be directed my way
This dance I have done. It is not a dance I choose.
I pray you will claim your anger and find the power within it
If you think its about standing up to me, know this is about standing up to your own ego and standing in your Self.
I do not feel loved by you
For if you truly loved yourself, you would not hurt me
You would heal the hurt within you, to take you out of your pain.
Being responsible means developing your ability
To respond to the pain, love, sorrow, wisdom and clarity within side of you.
Become One as a man.

Rose Buds Into Blossoms

The crash of the waves
Resound in the conversation
We had when you told me
That the truth I had spoken
Felt like thorns into your heart
I wondered when you were going
To take out the spiked tips
That punctured your calm finesse
From stillness and silence
Into awakened presence
You have transformed before my eyes
Watching you surrender
Has turned love into ecstasy
Rose buds into blossoms
To cover our bed in
And make love to you
Through the night.

Uniting Heaven and Earth

She returned
Through the veil
As One
Turning back one last
Time to view the universe
The stars danced
In light before her
He took off of his cloak
That he wore as his protection
Travelling through time and space
Into worlds beyond
He listened to meter and beat
Of his connection
To the source
Dancing with the sun and the rainbows
They create
Unveiling his power
He shone as a tower
A bringer of a new way
Where systems of separation
Have become One
They tune their rhythms
Raise up the light
Carry darkness to transform
In their love
They return home to their abode
As dawn shifts their way
From translucency to connectivity
Compassion
Holds open the door

For heaven and earth
To become One
Once again.

Live as the Flame

In all ways
The light
Shines through you
It cannot be stopped
For it cannot be destroyed
After the fire has burnt away all
Give thanks
For the remaining charcoals
They too shall become ash
From your nothingness
Grows the undestructable tree of life
Rooted in your BEing
As you end feeding the darkness
Do not withdraw
Into the nothingness
But sit in the space inbetween
The pain
This pain has created the crevice
Go into its opening
Of your discomfort
Embrace it
Embrace it again
Kiss the flames
Burning you some more
You will not die in its blaze
But only rise into its path of the phoenix
Living as the flame itself
All, nothing, nothing and all
Lighting the thunder
Crackling in its roar

Opening to the earth
Become the call
Live in the fire
The Light of your all
Let it take you over
Until you only feel the heat of love's passion
Reconstructing you at your core
Then dance the fire
May your heart become the ocean
And your body become the earth
As you merge into the sky
Into the final call to be fully loved
Give your heart to the burn of love
And let it build your desire
Know the God in you will take you over
As you breath life into the fire.

Lightning Power

I am the listener in your heart
Raging to set you free
The tidal waves make me believe
That your lightning power has you see
Each cell of your unknown
Opening you
To calm all your disbelieves
I am not afraid
When you try to unleash yourself so intensely
That I can become imprisoned by your passion
Light scent
Magic source
Enter me in streams of ecstasy
Blackened streams tremble me
For I know they are being released from you
Because of our belief in God together
I am the listener in your heart
Raging to set you free
The tidal waves make me believe
That your lightning power has you see
Each cell of your unknown
Opening you
To calm all your disbeliefs.

Seeds of Honesty

All paths lead here
Foreign only to your ears
Travel the wheel of time
Bound past all of hearts crimes
I am planting seeds of honesty
Standing clear this night
Waiting an eternity
As my body lives what is right
Moving past the fright.
Divinely living in the light
See me now
Blazing before you
Cast through souls ruin
Release my golden mire
I am the heart on fire
Loving you as deeply as I can
Leaping
Running
Opening the doorways
Into your arms
Be the God
Inside you
Make real
Loves reunion
I am planting seeds of honesty
Standing clear this night
Waiting an eternity
As my body lives what is right
Moving past the fright
Divinely living in the light

We have forgotten who we are
Warrioress's and Warrior's of the new
One in lights power
Taking back what is ours
Remember the prophecy
Of the tablets once known
Take off fake crowns
Sweet roses
Light the sound
I am planting seeds of honesty
Standing clear this night
Waiting an eternity
As my body lives what is right
Moving past the fright
Divinely living in the light.

Spirit's Flame

Two flowers, two mountains, two streams,
One moon, One sun
One beginning, One ending
The wind is silent as the word speaks
Through the faith of One heart
Blossoming in Spirit's flame
On this spring eve
The power of creation, rebirth, new vision rests
In the cradle of truth
One heart, One love, One eye, One voice
We celebrate all life
The laughter
Of our hearts
Beckon us home
Into the ecstasy of Light's passion and tenderness
The smile of God's power
Exploding our limitations
Resistance undone
Returns us to the kingdom
BEing given divine blessings
The union of Oneness
Enlightens our way
Loving
The allness
Lit by its
Blazing embrace
From God's chamber to our chamber
Its nectar
Guiding the way
The magnificence of passion at our feet

Giving praises to the One
From my One heart to your One heart
Opening to all remembrance
Embracing the seed of perfect union
Restoring life's creation
Our bodies singing love
We are birthed
As One flame
Of light
Joining the moon and the sun.

Sea of Tears

Your dreams left me in a sea of tears
For they were not mine
And had me believing
I could not fly.

Waiting Within the Center

She danced and sang
The rivers of eternity through her blood
Unknown outcomes
Known path emerging
Of truth and freedom
Being the currents that fearlessly
Crack through and break open
The walls of resistance
Surrounding the heart
Wounded man
Wounded woman
The lessons
Needed to shatter your ego
Will take you to your knees
If you are lucky enough
Blessed through your tears
To be given the grace needed
To merge into the yoke of consciousness
Waiting within the center of
Your wound
Here where your breath inhales
Exhaling all that is stagnant within you
End making up the rules
That keep you caught between
Your wound and God within
The light of your heart.

Welcoming His Cobra

As she drops her soul
Into the bucket of semen
The darkness opens to light
Her man having endured
The womb of pain
Is confused by the sudden
Change in scenery
He welcomes her embrace
As the strings of sadness
Are torn from his chest
Clinging to the pain
For the last time
He jumps through the veil
Into the unknown
Inviting him to
Leave the story
In his head
That he cannot live
As the Akhmenten king
Without the flirtations
Of a thousand women
Beckoning him in many forms
To be theirs
Amidst their hungry emptiness
He awakens through the dream
Of the feminine web
His spine turning to gold
The staff of life
Is returned
To him

By his cobra's enlightenment
Waiting for him
At the side door
Viewing his readiness
For the descent.

Cupids Gift

Liquid love
Caresses us in streams
Of gold
Alas centuries apart
We reunite
Shedding skins of anger, pain, and loss
We enter the central sun
Of light
Received by Ancient Ones
We are asked to release
Burdens and attachments
Fears to be absorbed by divine mother
And walk towards a new life
That is ready to be lived
Drenched in rose petals
Of joy
We hold each other
As night turns into day
Welcoming our love
Through ocean waves
Of kisses
That pull us home
Into the One.

With Your Touch

Each silent breeze
Passes through the window
Radiating my skin
With your touch
Your thoughts flow
Through my heart
As a cello motions
My body to breathe in life
Waiting for you
To hold
My hips with your hands
I give in to your mouth
Ravishing me
As a snakes belly
Merges with the earth
Imprinting the sun
With its spiral
Like tongue
Licking the salt
From the sweat on my back
You pound like the waves
Of the sea
Entering my shore
The cave opens
To receive your message
Of love.

Waiting for the Stars

I awaken
Your heart next to mine
Sings
Welcoming
A new day
Stripped of all pretenses
I roll on to you
Our thighs
Touching as leaves on a branch
Hum to the wind
Setting fire
A desire
As warm as a summer night
Waiting for the stars
To burst open
Their petals of light
Shining eternity on our path
We stand silently
Beholding
The gifts we have been given
Helping us to recognize
True love
As a passage rite
Out of anguish into bliss.

Moon

Moon in my eyes
I could never forget
How you look into eternity
Through my body.

Moon in my eyes
I whimper in desire
To feel your tongue
On mine.

Moon in my eyes
Only the cold ring
Of winter
Pulls you apart from me.

Moon in my eyes
There is no relief
From the torment
Felt when you become dark
And new.

Moon in my heart
There is no escape
As I let you in the door
To my soul.

Where the sun
Can penetrate
And create

Each day to
BE a new beginning
To set us free.

Pain to Bliss

When winter came in our hearts
I could no longer hear
The song of creation
Humming through you
Only the disruption
Of your fathers voice
Takes control of his
Stripped sons soul
He radically controlled
To make his
Over lifetimes
What did you think
Was yours
To bend, structure and recast
Into iron and then steel
Mistakenly created as yours
Your bliss would come
From soothing the suffering
Pain created from your broken heart
Realizing power and love
Were not separate
Many came and went
From your bed
Now waiting for you
The clean sheets
Spread smooth
Wondering if the torn
Tyrant is ready to let go
Of looking for bliss
Without responsibility

Or liability
The new king of light
Has no idea
How to find
And grow
Real bliss
That only comes from sustaining
The magnificence of BEing
Found in true love
The past wrought
Without true meaning
Written in struggle, death, and ownership
Lust and greed
False power and pride
The wind of God
Comes as a gust
Of divine bliss
Waiting tonight
In love
I feel you
Determined to BE
The enlightened king.

Take This New Design

When the time came
For the waters to break
Your soul refused to remain
In the dark
Tired of chasing dreams
And mothering hearts
To fill
The void of leaving your Self
You sat in the light of the moon
Afraid of your shadow
You gave Him the power
To make your body his kingdom
Revolving in shame
He made you his blame
To hide in the corner
Where his cobwebs
Covered your brain
That blocked your ability
To feel
And to be real
Alone in the night
The woman of manic power
Comes to fill you with life
While stealing your core Self
The you that you did
Not know you had
The dark feminine disguises
Her Self
As light
Ready to die in your arms

Her life now worthless
Matches your belief
That unless you give over your
Soul
Your only value is only something
That can be sold and bought for a dime
Take this new design
The blueprint of your heart
Ready to make a new start
You can have it
Just for the price
Of admission
Your desire to BE free.

Time To Love Again

The two parts of you
Dance in tune
With suffering
Each one trying
To fulfill
The others desire
Of suppressing or giving over
The right to BE
When death is meant to happen
Existence dependent upon
War
Within the self
Self-hatred festers the lies
Told to trick the heart into
Thinking it matters
How do you show
The heart that it is beautiful
And deserves to exist
How do you include it
In a life where the mind
Is king
Do you over throw the king
Or stop empowering its will
Is holding on to divine will
Enough to come through the fire
Who is winning your war
What does love think
Put down your swords it says
Give everything to me
Stop and breathe into me

As me
Become me
Allow love
To break you through
Your desire to be what you
Can never be
A false statue of perfection
Caught in pure neglect
Of the essence within its stone
Crack away the hatred rock
Until you shake and shatter
From the blaze of direct sunlight
Finally coming through the clouds
Of your rib cage and belly
Take off the good boy
Suit of armor
That has suffocated your soul
And reduced your pride
To engaging with darkness and fear
As a way to protect where you choose
To live
Create a new home
From within your bones, blood and skin
Give over to the earth and her love
What you have used
To exist
Instead of your heart
To nurture your decaying soul
Who was made to feel
By your choices
That it could not
Should not
Exist as the man
That he is

The old image must die
For someone new inside
To BE reborn
By embracing your pain
And healing your shame
Its time to love again.

One in Desire As One

The paw prints of the tiger
Lay dry in the noonday sun
Sitting and waiting
With the pulse of the earth
You rejoice to have the stripes
Of the currents of life
Beating its heart
In the drum of time
Tiger you are One
Sounding silence
Within the rays of the moon
Your desire to run
Has been burnt
To ash
While BEing
Aligned in
Pure power
Through you I ripple
As you wait at the gate
To allow others into the void
I sit on your back
One in desire as One.

Passion To Merge

The young girl
Forgets who she is
As the flower of truth
Light blazes forth
From the heart of her soul
Becomes focus
Of those out of control
The power she yields
Strikes fear in the hearts
Allowed too near who
Disregard Her essence
And choose instead
To deconstruct
The perfect creation
That has enormous patience
For those who hate
Themselves
Without regret
At last love enters the gate
Who sees himself
With truth and claims His own pain
Beyond shame
He holds the door
Open for His woman
To birth Her power
Changing His heart
Forever to BE the lover
Of love
Upholding nothing
Except pure emptiness

That is ready to BE filled
In Her overflowing
Passion to merge
With His fire
And to know desire
Uplifting
In the waves
While the moon rises
Raising the sea
Consecrating their love
In the light
Of the rising sun.

She is Taken

Dripping in raindrops
The sweat off her face
Soaks the flowering nipples
Budding as geysers
Singing to the sun
She rolls with the lion
Nestled in leaves
Their love
Saturates longing
Waiting to remember
Passion beyond fear
Refusing to hold back
She is taken
By the winds of union
Forgetting separation
They lie naked
Upon the roots
Holding the voice
Of the tree
Calling their names
To BE free.

In Love

Released in the wind
The river
Grabs her heart
And returns
Her to the moss
Covered currents
Flowing from the cave
Of no desire
Entering the shrine
Of darkness
She pulls herself
Close to the cool earth
Feeling the water
Flowing over her body
She enters
The pure light
Of the eternal sun
Released by the fire
Of her passion
To know bliss
She balances remembrance
With surrender
And kisses the droplets
Of nectar swimming
To meet her empty mind
In love.

Drink Freely

When I least expect it
I become you
From the center of the mountain
Life flows through wildflowers
Calling in the light of summer
To celebrate the unending story
Of life giving
Itself as water
Freeing the ties
Of the past
Unraveling the chains
Of trinkets we have held onto
To decrease our ability to
Drink freely
Open your mouth
Let me drip life
Onto your tongue
Feel its nectar
Running through the channels
Of timeless love
Come home with me.

Finding The River Again

The river took her in its heart
Peeling off her bark
Crickets sang to remind her
To trust the hands of love
Undone returned to wetness
Undulations rang through her body
As cobwebs of time
Stirred her into shifting course
Finding the river again
Gave her purpose
To enter the rhythms of ecstasy
Until she had become one
With the sun
Shedding her skin
The song of her bones
Danced with the fire
Of the moon
Pulsating up her spine
She entered the bliss
Of your kiss.

In the Least Expected Moment

In the darkness
Before the dawn
The forest sits awake
Each moment can BE felt
Without a mistake
Perfectly in motion
The sun joins in
As the orchestra invites
Life to be born
As the music
Of the soul
Take off the wrapping
Keeping you astray
Strip off your reluctancy
Drip love between your lips
Make me forget
Who I am
Part the valley
Into passion
Come explore
Beyond the threshold
Of reason
Lose your Self
Find your Self
Take what you need
Walk naked
To your destination
Discover you cannot be found
Only lost
And given back to you

In the least expected moment
As love itself
Ground into dust
You will die knowing
I have always been you.

My Beloved

You stand before me
As you have come
A hundred times before
You have always known
Who I Am
Beyond my own knowing
You welcome me
I welcome you
What do I need to learn
I ask
BE true to you
Then you will be true to me
And I will take care of the rest.

I Have Always Loved You

There is a song
Sung in silence
Beyond the call
Of the wild heart
Sitting alone
In my cave
Free in the light
I invite you
To join me
In my home of transparency
And delight
Beyond motion
Embraced in creation
I come to you
Again.

All Night Long

The willow tree
Leans down to the earth
To remember who she is
A nest from above
Wraps her love
Around me
I give myself
To the space
Between my body
And the song
Of the wind
That calls me home
To you
I have waited my whole
Life to find you
Here in the womb within
The home I find in your arms
For you have become
My willow tree
Holding me
All night long.

Finding the Queen and King of the Night

The dark moon begins
The search for lovers
Who wait to unveil their mysteries
Over grown in golden grasses
Quivering in reflections
They lose themselves
In the milky way
Seeking the answers
Once left behind
They seek to find their way.

For hundreds of years
I have walked this way
Seeking the path
Of freedom
Through entering the sanctuary
Of my soul
Who has been cast aside
Wandering through valleys
Touching rivers and mountain ridges.

As the wind ignites my passion
While waiting and wondering
If my king
Will every come again
Sitting by the silhouette
Of his beloved mountain
He, the king sits on the earth
As black panthers plant their footprints
Into the rich soil around him

They hold his head and heart tonight
Helping him to recover from the greed of women
Who have taken everything that they can
From his frightened innocence
He holds on to the empty tree
Within himself
Shaking in the cold breeze
Tonight praying how to find
The true feminine
Who will not steal his soul.

In their desperate attempt
To live through his power
While keeping him dependent
Upon his role to quench
Their thirst that has been created
Through fearing the pain within
Their womb
They pretend to let go
Of control
By gaining control
Holding a man's balls
They give themselves the chance
Pretend they can conquer
The weaknesses inherited from
Mothers who weep and keep
Their daughters victim
To their chains
Of control now disguised
As love disembodied.

In the night
The king takes off of his chains
And crawls inside of the empty

Tree filling it with his own body wisdom
He sings to the earth
Mother asking her forgiveness to
Take him inside of her heart
His soul is retrieved
And now he can leave
Hiding inside his pain.

Queen of the night in her velvet
Robe comes to undress
Her soul of gold
To her king
Who has set himself free
To enter her temple of love
She returns to him
The key to BE
One as the eagle
Who knows how to protect
His kingdom
And gives to her
The heart of his love
For he has waited
Hundreds of years
To find the One
Who can build upon the earth
Strength and integrity
Given from the other side
To empower
The couple who can walk
Through the fire of pain
All the while BEing tested
To endure the trials
Needed to give all
And lose all

To be found worthy
Of true love
Honored as sacred
The earth and sky
Unite again
From deep within
The mist.

Sex Is

Mistaken to be
A substitute for love
Sex is
The expression of how
My heart
Opens to receive you
Forgotten as the bond
Of surrender
The God in me
Yearns to merge
With the God in you
Sex is
The buoyancy
Of the wave
That holds us
As fear attempts
To separate
Us as One
To BEing two.

Waiting For You

No matter how rough
The waters rise
You always walk next to me
Veiled pain
Hides our potential
To merge into each other
Your life was bought
By others who traded your love
For possession of your soul
Far away from you
I stand on a distant shore
Watching the fog
Roll in and out
Always waiting for you
To unlock the door
To the gold within you
I heave in sorrow
Of having you taken away
From me
Just as our love
Unites
I hold the love
Waiting for you to yearn
To have us again
The tide comes in
And takes you out
On the next wave
Of a past lovers
Grief of wanting you
Should I comfort your loss

Or replace the love
That you never had
And could not have
For she was never available
To you
One pull of a string
The puppet masters
From your past
Pull you into their web
So they can dive into the bud
Of your nectar
Drinking your sweetness
I roll over in the night
Realizing the divine flame
Was already blown out
By the one who entered you first
Call in your male protector
Instead of merging with the feminine
Who pretends to love you
But just uses you
To fill their holes
I wipe the dried blood
From your sword wounds
Long ago agony
That you forgot to love
And allowed to grow into hollow
Trees separate from his roots
Alienated from the breath of his life
The dead man grieves the loss
Of his life force
That he believed
Others needed and would use
Better than he could

It's time to stop judging
Your pain
As failures
Through time
Growing shame between your legs
Let your Self rise up
To meet the sky
Once again
Choose to be heaven bound
Now close the door to your past
And walk through the fog
To divine love
Waiting for you.

The Light Rises

Passion builds in the silence
Of the roaring fire
Found through looking
Into your heart
Where God's embrace
Dissolves the thorns
Of broken dreams
Your cobra has transmuted
Now into a universe
Within you
That translates
The presence of eternal life
As a pillar of joy
Always ready
To love and hold you
While the skins of falsity
Twisted intentions
The deceit of corrupting pain
Into a way of holding on to you
Even though you were ready to go
Pull out the roots
Keeping you beholden
To another woman's womb
Find yours
In the bottom
Of the darkened cave
That needs the light
To lift your aching heart
Beyond the constrictions
Of how your cobra restricts

Its Self the motion
To destroy the hypocrisy
Of illusion
As we look towards each others
Heart to restore the fallen
Icons within our mind
We surrender into the blue
Light rising
As we let go
In each other's arms.

Of Your Soul

As I see
The molten lava
Dried around your body
I sit with you
Singing the tune
Of your soul
Who rests within the casket
Of black rock
The warmth of your emerging
Love melts your sorrows
Into the earth
It cannot give up
On refinding the hidden
Gem resting within the fire pit
Of your soul
You sing to me
Through your kisses
Forever roaring its way
Into my heart
I will wait for you
On the cliff overlooking
The star lit sky
Under the milky way
Until we meet again.

In the Center of Our Love

The yoke that binds us
Seals the honey
Ray beyond light
Uniting
Our heart of one
Expect to ignite
The release
Of your emptiness
Once freed
Our goblet
Tumbles
Down the stairs
To its original
Source in the void
Of desire
To BE One
Once again
In the center
Where we had begun
In the center
Of our love.

Of the Earth

The symphony began
As you played
Your tongue
Upon my lips
Where the sound
Of life
Lifted me up
To meet your mouth
Upon the heart
Of life
Where the sound
Of the earth
Through my womb
Rose to create
A river of color
That I rode
As a wave
Through my spine
Over and over again
The symphony began
With the rainbow
Rays of radiant
Light ready to move
The earth into alignment
Through my breath
I surrendered
To you
As you took me home
Into your heart.

Into Light

When you opened
Your heart
You exploded
The veils between
Your fear and independence
Pride that had grabbed
You in the night
Would seduce you into fear
As you rolled over
To face the setting moon
I missed you
Each time that you went
Away after we came
Into the molten volcanic
Blaze of heat
That I have never tired of
Your kisses have become
Longer taking us beyond
The pain that you have
Hid behind so that I would
Never find you
Exposed into the light
Your soul ignites the fire
Of our love
Now, after many full moons
I still long
To have your chest against mine
As we enter the dream of love
That has become real
Our joy ignites your eyes in the fires

Of God
The resistance is gone
Our language of delight
Transforms the dream of love
Our legs entwined
We become One heart
No longer seeking
Love has captured
Us in its embrace and moans
Cradling us in a universe
That rocks our perceptions
Into the night cracking through
What we have known
To BE possible
Our bodies turn into love
As we transform the dream
Into light.

Face the Sun

She could never love
Who you actually are
You became trained to disappear
Blocking your tears
Cement walls to your pain
Rebuild themselves in mortar and love
Never allowing your heart
To expand beyond a certain point
You would always remain guarded
When your genitals were stroked
Without your permission
The remembrance of its intrusion
Created illusions of love
The one who allowed you to leave your body
Was the one you held onto
For comfort and joy
When will you let go
Of the security that you had
And turn to the light
Of a new dawn with me
Every stroke
Of your hand
Sends me home into ecstasy
Will you forgive your Self
For dissolving into the dark
Instead of the light
And holding on to the ones
Who need you as much
As the woman who birthed you
Yet could never protect you

From harm
Are you a woman seeking shelter
Are you a man refusing to let go
Waiting to be taken away
Into the earth's vibration
Of creation and birth
Why stay in the birth canal
When your soul is saying
Here is a new cloak of light
Move forward now and face the sun.

The Sacred Hoop

For eons of time
Our divine feminine of love
Has held the hoop
Of wisdom
She invites us
As a mother
And friend
To become One
With the currents of life
Pushing us to be born
Without strife
Torn from the fabric
Of Oneness
We are moved
To know our Selves
Beyond the weeping
Confusion of a child
Out at sea
How we take on the responsibility
To love our Self
Through the waves
Of pain and joy
We weep through the madness
To remember our true connection
The heart of Oneness
Always stand in your center
BE the flame of truth
Let go and fall through
The hoop of devotion
To the God within You.

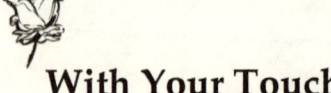

With Your Touch

In the holy sacred center
Of the heart
That you came here to give
Resides the joy
Free from pain
Yet embraces past shame
All that you are is received
In this moment
To give your Self
The freedom
To embrace who you are
Feel the currents
Of new beginnings
Where earth and heaven
Touch each other
Within the womb
Of your heart
Ready to give birth
To the Source
Of life
That is you
With your touch.

Ready To BE Born

In our world of confusion
Created by the fear of God
Being a separate corporate entity
With it own family rules
The need for sensuality
Is breaking all the rules
Abundant as the earth's lushness
Pushes through false and superficial
Lies created through ego's illusion
To subdiverge, analyze, identify and quantify
The pure heart of love
Which has been allowed
To be broken
Without a token of shame
By repressing and depressing the life force
Of God coming through the body
Naming its name
With a power to be seen and received
Instead of morality with no heart
Or cruelty sentenced to another living being
Because of a forgotten paralyzed heart
The roar of your sex
The song of its exuberance
The love it brings
Will conquer your fear
Of the life that you fear
Quenching the thirst
Exploding
From the voice of your soul
Ready to BE born

As your heart and your vagina
As your heart and your penis
Join in honor of the life
You have been given
Receive the initiation
Through the lips of the earth
Kissing your heart
To help you make a new start
Ready to BE Born.

The Soul As One

The Soul As One
Creates As One
The Heart in Two
Creates the Mind in Two
Sex As One
Brings Two As One
Tears As One
Reunites Two to One
Body Soul As One
Births One As One
Spirit Flesh in God
Burns As One
Lives in One.

May these GODSEX poems of divine union
continue to ignite and inspire the journey of
your body, heart, and soul to unite through
the eternal love of divine sexuality.

To learn more about Iana Lahi, the Creative
and Executive Director of Spirit Gateways®
Institute, Spirit Gateways® Education, &
Spirit Gateways® Leadership go to:

ianalahi.com

www.ingramcontent.com/pod-product-compliance
Lightning Source LLC
Chambersburg PA
CBHW060355080526
44583CB00012B/319